We have no eternal allies, and we have no perpetual enemies. Our interests are eternal, and it is our duty to follow them.

British Prime Minister Henry John Temple, Lord Palmerston, in a speech to the House of Commons, March 1, 1848

IT'S NOT OFTEN that we get a glimpse into Barack Obama's mind. In 2008, Samuel Wurzelbacher – A.K.A. "Joe the Plumber" – fell into one when his question to then-presidential candidate Obama about taxes resulted in the famous "spread the wealth around" answer, revealing Obama's redistributionist economic beliefs.

And, at the close of his flashy multinational nuclear "summit," Barack Obama had another "Joe the Plumber" moment.

Speaking of Middle Eastern conflicts, Obama said, "It is a vital national security interest of the United States to reduce these conflicts because whether we like it or not, we remain a dominant military superpower, and when conflicts break out, one way or another

[1]

we get pulled into them. And that ends up costing us significantly in terms of both blood and treasure."

Not that America is rightfully proud of its ability to protect ourselves and our allies, to protect freedom, and pursue our interests around the world. Not that we are a force for good. "Whether we like it or not, we remain a dominant military superpower."

Not that we will defend our freedom-loving allies from aggression, but "when conflicts break out, one way or another we get pulled into them."

President Obama does not believe we have the right or the obligation to influence other nations, protect our allies, and pursue our interests abroad. After more than a year of reducing the future capabilities of our military and intelligence communities, his administration's actions make it clear that he seeks to end America's role as a global superpower.

It's wrong to accuse Barack Obama of naivete. The consistency with which he and Secretary of Defense Robert Gates have acted to reduce the capability of our armed forces – now and in the future – defines his objective: to reduce America from a superpower to an also-ran, a nation that is incapable of defending its interests or its allies around the world.

He may think of himself as the "un-Bush," but in historical context, he is the "un-Palmerston." At the top of Obama's agenda is to transform our military and intelligence capabilities from those of a superpower to the claws of a paper tiger.

The proofs are comprehensive.

Casting the Pentagon's future not in steel but in glass, Obama and Gates have reduced

---

President Obama does not believe we have the right or the obligation to influence other nations, protect our allies, and pursue our interests abroad.

---

or eliminated most of the key weapon systems – ranging from the F-22 fighter to the Navy's DDG-1000 stealthy combatant ship – which would have maintained the technological superiority that our forces have depended on since Korea to win quickly and decisively on the modern battlefield.

They are delaying the purchase of the most urgently needed tool for maintaining our superpower abilities – the Air Force's replacement for the Eisenhower-era KC-135 airborne tanker – to allow the makers of the French-made Airbus A330 to compete, despite its physical inability to perform the mission.

They have reduced our missile defense program and abandoned the defense of Europe. They have promised, instead of the anti-missile defenses based in Poland, a sea-based system that they know cannot be deployed in the foreseeable future.

Obama says he wants to rid the world of nuclear weapons. But instead of moving decisively against Iran's nuclear ambitions, he has revised our nuclear doctrine to reduce the value of our deterrent and has prevented the modernization of our nuclear arsenal, leaving its effectiveness in doubt.

Obama and his congressional allies want to reengineer the military culture, repealing the "Don't Ask, Don't Tell" law that prevents homosexuals from serving openly in the military. He and Gates have already rescinded the rule that prohibited women from serving on submarines. Both of those initiatives will hurt morale and readiness of our forces to fight.

OBAMA'S WAR AGAINST
THE INTELLIGENCE COMMUNITY

Nothing will hurt more – or cost more lives sooner – than Obama's war against our intelligence community.

There is insufficient room here to fully explain that war. A few examples suffice.

One of Obama's first acts upon taking office was to ban the "enhanced interrogation techniques" (EITs) used successfully on al Qaeda bigs during the Bush administration. That action cut off the single most valuable source of intelligence on terrorist activities. Of the EIT program, former CIA Director George Tenet wrote, "What [the terrorist detainees] gave us was worth more than the CIA, NSA, the FBI and our military operations had achieved collectively." By ending the use of the EITs, Obama has made us more vulnerable to terrorist attacks.

In pre-confirmation meetings with Republican senators, Attorney General Eric Holder promised he would not seek prosecution of CIA interrogators who had used the EITs. But after a reported profanity-laced screaming match with CIA Director Leon Panetta at the White House, Holder broke that promise.

House Speaker Rep. Nancy Pelosi (D-Calif.) has helped break the bond of trust that must exist between the White House and our spies. Resisting allegations that she had known that waterboarding was being used on al Qaeda terrorists while it was going on in 2002 and 2003, she accused the CIA of lying about briefing her. The CIA subsequently proved it was not lying by releasing summaries of contemporaneous documents. Nevertheless, Pelosi won that battle by refusing to recant her accusation, leading Panetta to write an unprecedented op-ed in *The Washington Post*.

In it, Panetta said there was "an atmosphere of declining trust, growing frustration and more frequent leaks of properly classified information." But Obama didn't support Panetta. Pelosi's accusation hangs in the air, just like Holder's ongoing "investigation" of CIA interrogators.

These blows to the CIA's morale were not healed. Instead, Obama made it worse by imposing perverse priorities on the intelligence agency. A prime example is his decision to make the study of global warming one of its assigned tasks. On Jan. 4, 2010, *The New York Times* reported that Obama had revived a program that requires the CIA to collaborate with "environmental scientists" to study climate change.

The Obama administration insists that the

CIA global warming study is "free," that it uses only satellite downtime and doesn't detract from the gathering or analysis of real intelligence information. But that contention is, at best, absurd.

Intelligence satellites – each of which costs upwards of $100 million – have a finite life. Every time they are repositioned, they use fuel that cannot be replaced. And every hour a CIA analyst spends examining radar images of a polar bear's behind is one less hour spent analyzing information that might reveal where Osama bin Laden is hiding or how close Iran may be to producing a nuclear warhead.

Without the best intelligence and analysis, policy making is mere guesswork. And our intelligence is woefully inadequate.

In August 2006, the Republican staff of the House Permanent Select Committee on Intelligence released a special report that severely criticized the CIA and other intelligence agencies for lacking "the ability to acquire essential information necessary to make judgments" on Iran's nuclear weapon program.

Almost four years later, nothing has improved. Gates, the former CIA director and current secretary of defense, admitted on NBC's April 11, 2010, *Meet the Press* that while Iran isn't now "nuclear capable," if it gains that capability, we won't be able to know if it is converting nuclear capability into nuclear arms.

The inescapable inference is that even if the Iranians prove to the world that they are

---

Every hour a CIA analyst spends examining radar images of a polar bear's behind is one less hour spent analyzing information that might reveal where Osama bin Laden is hiding or how close Iran may be to producing a nuclear warhead.

---

able to build nuclear weapons, we don't have the ability to know whether or not they are building them. But it's OK to divert scarce intelligence assets to study global warming.

Is "Next-War-itis" a Mental Disease?

From the Revolutionary War through Korea, it has been America's unfortunate tradition to be unprepared for war. In both World Wars and Korea, we went to war with the weapons, strategies, and tactics of the previous war. It's not our experience alone. The French, for example, built the Maginot Line to repel the German Army of World War I, but only after that war was over. By 1940, the Luftwaffe and Wehrmacht of World War II had evolved past 1918.

After Korea, we belatedly took George Washington's admonition to heart. In his first annual address to Congress in 1790, Washington said, "To be prepared for war is one of the most effective means of preserving peace." And we did it with a history-making investment that produced a constant flow of new technologies. Because our economy was so strong, we could and did invest in the men and machines that would dominate any modern battlefield. Our military and intelligence community was led by people who jumped on opportunities to advance those technologies. I was privileged to know some of these men.

In the late 1980s, while working for Lockheed Corporation, I was befriended by an irascible genius by the name of Ben Rich. (He liked to say that around Lockheed's supersecret "Skunk Works," he was known as "FBR" and that the "F" wasn't for "friendly.") A thermodynamicist by trade, Rich apprenticed with the great Kelly Johnson, and by the time I met him, he was the head of the Skunk Works.

Rich – and his intelligence community customers – were the varsity team of technology jumpers, always looking for something that would leapfrog whatever the Soviets (or anyone else, for that matter) were doing.

Like others who keep our nation's most closely guarded secrets, Ben was garrulous about what little he could say in public. He told me one story that is an example of how we propelled the technologies that enabled our forces to dominate the modern battlefield.

Rich had participated in the development of our nation's premier reconnaissance aircraft, the U-2 and the SR-71 Blackbird, the fastest aircraft ever built. Consequently, he had a very good relationship with the Air Force and the intelligence agencies that were the principal customers of the work those aircraft did. They often sent him translations of foreign technical journals.

One Sunday morning, Rich was sitting in his bathrobe, coffee on his lap and a cigarette in his mouth, reading a Russian journal of mathematics. He came across a small item about a Russian who claimed that he'd proven an equation that would, by including an unusual set of defined variables that describe an object's shape, compute the size of the image it would project on radar. And there it was in black and white.

Rich told me he jumped up from the sofa,

spilling coffee and scattering papers all around the room as he bolted to his telephone. Later that day, he and his engineering staff were working to satisfy themselves with the Russian's work. And as soon as they did, he was on the way to an unnamed government agency's headquarters to explain how he could build a stealthy aircraft. Thus was born the top-secret Have Blue program, which – as we learned much later – became the F-117A stealth fighter.

GATES AND "NEXT-WAR-ITIS": THE PENTAGON HAS THE "HAVE BLUE BLUES"

Team Obama shuns that kind of technological investment.

In 2008, while serving as George W. Bush's secretary of defense, Robert Gates said, "I have noticed too much of a tendency towards what might be called 'Next-War-itis' – the propensity of much of the defense establishment to be in favor of what might be needed in a future conflict."

Gates believes that in the new multipolar world, there is no reason to worry about another conventional war. In that speech, he also said that "it is hard to conceive of any country confronting the United States directly in conventional terms – ship to ship, fighter to fighter, tank to tank – for some time to come." He and Obama see no need to invest in future weapons and research because – to them – another conventional war is unthinkable.

Gates apparently believes "next-war-itis" is a mental disorder. He and President Obama are busy curing the Pentagon of "next-war-itis" by abandoning the advancement of military technologies.

Gates's thinking is comprehensively wrong for two reasons.

First, even in the war against terrorists, conventional weapons are essential.

The most urgent radio call in any theater of battle is "troops in contact," meaning U.S. ground forces are in a firefight with terrorists. In Afghanistan and Iraq, that call brings the

Gates and Obama see no need to invest in future weapons and research because — to them — another conventional war is unthinkable.

Air Force and Navy fighters and attack aircraft — the "fast movers" — into the fight as quickly as they can get there. Their precision-guided weapons often prove to be the difference between life and death for our troops on the ground.

Second, our potential adversaries don't agree with Gates, and their vote will be decisive. China, Russia, North Korea, and Iran are all engaged in frantic efforts — separately and together — to build technologically advanced military forces that can prevent American forces from interfering in their military ambitions.

China is the best example. They are spending a far higher percentage of their gross domestic product than we are on advanced weapon systems.

One vital component of our technological superiority is the constellation of satellites we have in orbit today. American forces are almost entirely dependent on those satellites for communication, navigation, and intelligence. Without them, our aircraft, ships, missiles, and precision-guided munitions are essentially blind.

To ensure a decisive advantage over us, China is building anti-satellite weapons. In a landmark 2007 test, they downed one of their old satellites with a kinetic-kill vehicle, hitting a bullet with a bullet. In 2006, they tested a directed-energy weapon that could rapidly blind or destroy satellites in great numbers.

To capitalize on their advantage, the Chinese are also building microsatellites that can be prepared and launched quickly in the event we use anti-satellite weapons against theirs.

China's military strategy now includes

"local wars under conditions of informatization." That means the Chinese have a strategy that is based on electronic warfare, ranging from communications jamming to the most advanced methods of cyberwarfare. They have the capability – as they demonstrated more than a year ago – to invade and interfere in American computer networks. The demonstration, as several sources have told me, was an interruption of the U.S. Army's Pentagon-based e-mail system.

In its 2009 report on China's military power, the Department of Defense said:

China has or is acquiring the ability to: 1) hold large surface ships, including aircraft carriers, at risk (via quiet submarines, advanced anti-ship cruise missiles (ASCMs), wire-guided and wake-homing torpedoes, or anti-ship ballistic missiles); 2) deny use of shore-based airfields, secure bastions and regional logistics hubs (via conventional ballistic missiles with greater ranges and accuracy, and land attack cruise missiles); and, 3) hold aircraft at risk over or near Chinese territory or forces (via imported and domestic fourth generation aircraft, advanced long-range surface-to-air missile systems, air surveillance systems, and ship-borne air defenses).

These developments are planned specifically to counter U.S. forces and to deny them the ability to enter the theater of battle to intervene to help defend Japan, Taiwan, and the other nations that the Chinese believe should be encompassed in their hegemony.

The Chinese are developing their own stealthy aircraft. And the Russians are in a partnership with India to develop a fifth-generation fighter to compete with our F-22.

Russia is also developing anti-satellite weapons and has demonstrated its cyberwar capabilities. In the spring of 2007, Russia unleashed a series of cyber attacks against Estonia, a former Soviet satellite, effectively preventing Estonia's government from functioning.

On May 10, 2010, the Obama administration announced the formation of a U.S. Cyber Command headquartered in the National

Security Agency. Are we far behind China and Russia?

"Next-war-itis" isn't a mental disorder; it's a recognition of reality. And here's the choice: Embrace "next-war-itis" or decide to sink in the 21st century equivalent of the Maginot Line mentality. There's no third option.

It takes at least a decade to put a new fighter in the air and as long or longer to develop and build a new Navy combatant ship. It may take a lot longer to create defensible satellites or computer defenses against what the Chinese – and other nations – are developing.

If you don't plan a decade ahead – and invest in the technologies you need – you risk losing too many lives or even losing a war.

To cure America's military of "next-war-itis," President Obama and Gates made drastic cuts in current and future weapon systems without any analytical basis to justify them.

Reducing the defense budget by $30 billion in 2010, they included cuts to the next generation of military technologies, which freeze our abilities at mid-1980s levels.

It has been 57 years since an American ground soldier was killed by an enemy aircraft. Air supremacy has been the birthright of every American soldier since 1953. It means complete protection against enemy aircraft and the availability of close air support delivered by fast-moving aircraft.

To protect Japan, South Korea, Taiwan, and Israel, air supremacy must be achieved instantly, and the best missile defenses must be deployed in sufficient numbers – and with

---

If you don't plan a decade ahead – and invest in the technologies you need – you risk losing too many lives or even losing a war.

---

sufficient technological capability – to defeat the constantly evolving missile threat.

Constant technological progress is the

only path to reliably achieving air supremacy in the future. But Obama and Gates don't believe in it. Scoffing at the supersonic stealthy F-22 Raptor, Gates and Obama ended its production at 187 aircraft.

The original Air Force plan was to buy 750 Raptors to replace the 1970s vintage F-15, our current top-line fighter. With the demise of the Soviet Union, the requirement was reduced in successive administrations to what the Air Force said was a "moderate risk" force of about 250 F-22s that were needed to meet operational requirements.

But if 250 F-22s is a "moderate risk," the cut to 187 means an even higher risk that an enemy can challenge U.S. air supremacy in a future war.

Obama and Gates are increasing the risk of defeat in conventional war by substituting the less-capable F-35 for the F-22.

The F-35 is the Obama-Gates choice for the future of the Air Force, Navy, and Marines. But the F-35 isn't designed to perform the air superiority mission; the F-22 is. The F-22 can perform combat maneuvers at 50,000 feet; the F-35 can't do so at altitudes in excess of 30,000 feet. The F-22 has an integrated combat system, allowing it to link its on-board sensors (radar and more) to external sensors on the ground and in space. The F-35 can't.

All of this adds up to a current – and continuing – shortage of fighter aircraft for both the Air Force and the Navy.

According to the Congressional Research Service, the Air Force is forecasting a fighter shortfall of 800 aircraft from 2017 to 2024 and a shortfall of about 240 for the Navy and Marine Corps.

This means that the Navy and Air Force expect to have too few aircraft to meet their operational needs now and for at least the next decade and a half. For our ground troops, it means that the "troops in contact" call may not be answered in time. To our allies, it means that they will be far more vulnerable.

And the shortfall will be worse than forecast, because the F-35 won't be there to make up the difference in performance or numbers.

Russia recently unveiled its Sukhoi T-50. Russians claim it is capable of supersonic cruise, can carry an impressive array of advanced weapons, and is invisible to radar. We are supposed to take comfort in Obama and Gates's belief that we'll never have to fight another "conventional" war.

That Obama and Gates shun advanced technology doesn't just affect the Air Force. The Navy's stealthy DDG-1000 combat ship program was also terminated.

Naval combatant forces have, since World War II, been deployed en masse. Carrier battle groups – a dozen or more ships – were sent all over the world to protect allies and attack enemies. Naval air forces, operating from carriers, have been crucial in Iraq and Afghanistan. But Obama and Gates are cutting the carrier groups from 11 to 10.

And while they are doing that, they have rejected the DDG-1000, a highly advanced ship that was designed to operate alone in remote corners of the world. The DDG-1000 was to be equipped with a breakthrough technology: Raytheon's AN/SPY-3 multifunction radar, which is designed to detect and track low-observable cruise missiles and support anti-missile missiles such as the Standard series, now relied on for fleet protection.

The DDG-1000 was designed for littoral warfare – to fight, alone if need be, in remote areas where it is necessary to run close to shore. This is the sort of weapon system we should build. Its capabilities in conventional and unconventional warfare could provide a decisive advantage in the China Sea or the Persian Gulf.

Instead of the 12 DDG-1000s the Navy needs, we will build only three.

The Army hasn't escaped the Obama-Gates crusade against new technologies. Beginning in 1999, it began developing its Future Combat Systems program, an integrated series of unmanned ground and air vehicles and a new highly advanced battle management system.

But in early 2009, Obama and Gates canceled Future Combat Systems. The Army is now going back to plan a new system to satisfy them, directed at counterterrorist limited warfare.

Obama and Gates Are Cutting Investment in Current Forces and Playing Politics with Key Systems

It took the French about 14 years to build their carrier, the *Charles de Gaulle.* They did have their problems; for example, a propeller fell off in the first sea trial, and they had to rebuild the flight deck when they realized it was too short to operate the aircraft they'd planned to deploy on the ship.

We don't suffer from French engineering, but unless political influence is taken out of the game, we will take as long or longer to replace the Air Force's aged KC-135 tanker fleet.

Tankers aren't sleek and sexy like fighters; they're big and boring. The KC-135, an Eisenhower-era Boeing 707 modified for airborne refueling of every aircraft in the Air Force inventory, was built to last about 25 years. The fleet – about 534 aircraft – is now on average 46 years old.

Tankers may be boring but – as then-Air Force Chief of Staff Gen. John Jumper told me in a 2005 interview – without them, America isn't a superpower. Jumper said, "We are a global air and space power because of these tankers." Why? "The first thing that happens in any contingency is that you put the tanker bridge up there. We deploy tankers to places such as Spain, Hawaii, Guam, and their sole purpose is to get large numbers of transport aircraft halfway around the world without stopping." The same goes for combat aircraft of all types and sizes.

I've been writing about the tanker crisis since Sept. 15, 2003. In my first article, which appeared in *National Review Online*, I wrote, "Some 22 percent of the KC-135Es – about 120 of them – are now under operational restrictions, meaning they can't fly most combat missions. Only about 38 of our KC-135Es were able to fly in Operation Iraqi Freedom." In the almost seven years since then, the problem has gotten worse.

One attempt at buying a replacement tanker failed when Boeing was embroiled in a major scandal centering on an Air Force civilian employee whom it had bribed with a job offer. A second round was undone when the Air Force broke its own rules by choosing a French aircraft that was unsuitable to the mission. The problem now is politics.

Boeing has offered a tanker version of its 767 airliner. This is all well and good, because the 767 is capable of performing the mission without causing extraneous problems such as rebuilding runways to hold its weight. But the European Aeronautic Defense and Space Company (EADS) has been – for years – pushing the Airbus A330 in competition with the Boeing aircraft.

In 2008, the Air Force awarded the contract to a Northrop Grumman/EADS consortium, but Boeing had the award thrown out by protesting to the Government Accountability

Office. The GAO found that the Air Force had ignored some of the physical problems with the Airbus that should have disqualified it.

Problems include the fact that the Airbus's top speed is too low (perhaps as low as 380 MPH, versus the Boeing's 530 MPH top speed, according to public sources), can't accelerate fast enough to perform mandatory safety maneuvers while refueling, and is so bloody big that the Air Force will have to spend hundreds of millions rebuilding runways and hangars to house it. According to the experts I've interviewed, the Airbus is so big that other aircraft – fighters and such – will have to be moved to other bases, because the Airbus takes up too much room on the parking ramps. (And that's not the end of it. The A330 has the same tail assembly that has broken off the A300 airliner several times during sudden maneuvering, killing hundreds of people. But I digress.)

To the Europeans, any effort by the Air Force to enforce the standards it has developed over more than 50 years of in-flight refueling boils down to American protectionism. They insist – and Sen. John McCain has bullied the Pentagon into accepting their position – that the price of the Airbus can't be adjusted to balance the playing field for Boeing. Airbus receives hundreds of millions of dollars in "launch aid" subsidies that the World Trade Organization ruled last year were illegal.

Right now, the Air Force is about to start yet another round of competition to contract for the replacement of the KC-135 tankers. If Obama and Gates were interested in getting the best aircraft for our fliers, they would order the Pentagon to eliminate the Airbus and wire brush Boeing in a tough negotiation to get the right aircraft, as soon as possible, at the best price.

Instead, they have delayed the contract process to allow EADS – now without its partner Northrop Grumman, which dropped out last year – enough time to cobble up a bid. The French government, which recently turned Obama down flat for reinforcements for Afghanistan, is undoubtedly pressuring the White House to give EADS a more than fair opportunity.

Either way, our fliers lose. They may yet get the Boeing KC-767, delayed for years to come. Or they will get the Airbus, the too-slow, too-big, and unsafe-at-any-speed aircraft, to please the French. No tankers, no superpower. And if you want to cripple the superpower, what better way than to buy a tanker aircraft that cannot perform the mission in accordance with Air Force standards?

In a May 2010 speech, Gates said, "The attacks of September 11, 2001, opened a gusher of defense spending that nearly doubled the base budget over the last decade.... The gusher has been turned off, and will stay off for a good period of time."

The Air Force now has 77 B-52s. They will be 100 years old when they are retired, according to current plans. There is no long-range bomber on the drawing boards to replace it. The "gusher" may be off for a long period of time, but it won't be a good period.

We will wait, behind Gates's virtual Maginot Line, for the next war to come to us.

Obama's Missile Defense Scam

Obama claims that he is moving forward with anti-missile defense systems. But his actions are delaying some programs, canceling others, and leaving our allies with broken promises.

According to The Heritage Foundation, President Obama's 2010 defense budget cut $1.4 billion from the Missile Defense Agency. They scaled back the Airborne Laser boost-phase program, terminated the Multiple Kill Vehicle and Kinetic Energy Interceptor, canceled the expansion of ground-based inter-

---

We will wait, behind Gates's virtual Maginot Line, for the next war to come to us.

---

ceptors in Alaska and California, and delayed funding for interceptor and radar sites in Poland and the Czech Republic.

The budget for 2011 was better. The Alaska-based missile interceptors were reduced from 44 to 30 in 2010. Now the number is back up to 38. And Obama has added an upgrade to three Aegis ships to ballistic missile defense capability. But those increases, especially in the Aegis ship upgrades, aren't enough to make up for the damage he's done.

Poland – a staunch American ally before and after the Cold War – braved renewed Russian enmity by agreeing to host a ground-based ballistic missile defense system. Last year, Obama abruptly canceled it.

Defense Secretary Gates said Obama's plan was supposed to replace, on an equal basis, the land-based system and still mollify Russia. Under that plan, we would deploy at least three Navy Aegis-equipped ships carrying SM-3 interceptor missiles in the Mediterranean Sea in 2011 and possibly add land-based interceptors in 2015. Obama and Gates said the seaborne defenses could be deployed more quickly and would cost less.

But that promise is a false one. We have too few ships to accomplish it.

The Navy has about 80 Aegis-equipped ships, but only about 21 of them are configured for fleet missile defense, and only a handful of those are capable of reequipping for ballistic missile defense. All of the 21 are fully engaged in protecting our fleet around the world or are on call to protect allies such as Japan, as well as U.S. ground forces in the Middle East and elsewhere.

You can't just flip a switch and convert a fleet missile defense ship to ballistic missile defense. To convert them to ground defense, the ships have to sail home to exchange computer software and missiles designed to intercept low-flying cruise missiles for others designed for high-altitude ballistic missile intercepts.

Even if Obama wants to take three Aegis ships away from protecting U.S. forces, nine ships, not three, are required in order to have three on station at all times. If three are standing guard constantly in the Mediterranean, you need at least six more to be able to rotate the three home for refitting, crew retraining, and rest.

Obama's promise to Poland is illusory. The Poles know it, the Russians know it, and our Navy knows it.

Nuclear Dreamer

President Obama has often said that his goal is to eliminate nuclear weapons in the world. But while North Korea partners with Iran to develop and build nuclear weapons, the only reductions in nuclear weaponry – and the doctrine enabling their use – are ours.

Obama has taken two major steps to reduce the value of our nuclear deterrent: in his April 2010 Nuclear Posture Review and in the new nuclear arms reduction treaty with Russia, which now faces Senate confirmation.

The United States has not conducted an underground nuclear test since September

1992. Our nuclear arsenal (consisting, according to a startling revelation by Secretary of State Hillary Clinton, of 5,113 weapons) is aged and may be unreliable. For more than a decade, Pentagon experts have been clamoring for the design of a new, reliable weapon. Some insist that we resume underground tests to ensure the reliability of the weapons.

But Obama's Nuclear Posture statement ends the possibility of either. On April 6, 2010, he said, "The United States will not conduct nuclear testing and will seek ratification of the Comprehensive Test Ban Treaty. The United States will not develop new nuclear warheads or pursue new military missions or new capabilities for nuclear weapons."

And he went on to make a surprising change in U.S. nuclear doctrine. Every other president – using the threat of nuclear retaliation as a deterrent – has intentionally kept vague our doctrine regarding when we would retaliate to a non-nuclear attack with nuclear weapons. But Obama devalued our deterrent by changing the rules.

Under Obama's new doctrine, we will not use nuclear weapons in response to chemical, biological, or cyber attacks – regardless of the number of casualties – if the perpetrating nation is not known to be nuclear armed and is compliant with the Nuclear Non-Proliferation Treaty.

In one statement, Obama devalued our deterrent and made it hostage to, of all institutions, the United Nations. The U.N.'s International Atomic Energy Agency is, after all, the final arbiter of compliance with the nuclear treaty. But the agency is, to say the least, an unreliable judge of the facts. It has been a purblind watchdog and chief apologist for Iran for more than 20 years.

In early May 2010, Obama signed a new Strategic Arms Reduction Treaty with Russia. It is supposed to reduce each side's nuclear arsenal to 1,550 warheads and 700 delivery vehicles. This means the U.S. will have to destroy 70 percent of the warheads we now have: 3,563 of 5,113. And we will not modernize the ones left by replacing the old and possibly nonfunctioning warheads with new ones.

How many "delivery vehicles" will have to be scrapped as well?

The Air Force has 97 bombers – 77 B-52s and 20 B-2s – capable of carrying nuclear weapons. In addition, it has about 400 F-15s, some of which can be made nuclear capable, and about 450 Minuteman missiles. The Air Force also has almost 2,000 cruise missiles that are normally used with conventional weapons – as they were in both the Persian Gulf War in 1991 and in the Middle East since 2001 – but they could be considered nuclear capable.

The Navy's arsenal includes about 430 Trident D-5 intercontinental ballistic missiles on 18 *Ohio* class ballistic missile submarines. In addition, the Navy has about 3,000 cruise missiles that – like the Air Force's – are used with conventional warheads but could be considered nuclear delivery vehicles.

How many of these 6,395 aircraft, missiles,

and submarines does President Obama plan to scrap to get down to the magical number of 700 delivery vehicles?

The only good thing about the new treaty is that it is so vague and has so many collateral agreements that are still being negotiated that the Senate may refuse to ratify it. If they did, they'd be ratifying a blank sheet of paper.

Diversity Über Alles?

It's impossible for liberals to understand the military culture because so very few of them have served in uniform. They cannot be made to understand the dilemma it poses – how strong that culture is, yet how little it would take to destroy it.

But liberals don't really care. The concepts contained in the words "duty, honor, country" are abstractions to them. And they won't be satisfied until our military's culture is un-moored, left adrift in the political tide.

Bill Clinton wasn't in office a week before he signed an executive order attempting to overturn the prohibition of homosexuals serving in the military. He then spent months trying to back down and save face.

Neither the military nor senior congressional Democrats would support him. As a result, we got the 1993 law that permits homosexuals to serve, but only if they don't profess their homosexuality or practice it openly. And since then, it's been called "Don't Ask, Don't Tell."

President Obama campaigned against the law and has repeatedly promised it will be repealed. But the repeal of "Don't Ask, Don't Tell" is only one step Obama is taking to change the military culture.

It's impossible for liberals to understand the military culture because so very few of them have served in uniform.

Everything Obama is doing – ranging from Defense Secretary Gates's call to limit military pay and benefits to rescinding the rule against women serving on submarines and pushing for repeal of "Don't Ask, Don't Tell" – will damage the services' ability to recruit and retain the best soldiers, sailors, Marines, airmen, and Coast Guardsmen.

It's a volunteer force. If people don't want to serve, they don't have to. At this point, why would they?

After the Fort Hood shooting in 2009, Army Chief of Staff Gen. George Casey said, "Our diversity, not only in our Army, but in our country, is a strength. And as horrific as this tragedy was, if our diversity becomes a casualty, I think that's worse."

Why would anyone want to serve in an army whose leader believes it more important to be politically correct than to protect the lives of the soldiers from internal threats such as Maj. Nidal Malik Hasan, the alleged Fort Hood murderer?

Striking another blow in the name of diversity, in April 2010, Obama and Gates rescinded the Navy regulation prohibiting women from serving on submarines.

Navy families – especially the wives of submariners – sacrifice a lot. Their fathers, sons, and husbands are away at sea for long months. And it was primarily for the peace of mind of the wives whose husbands were at sea that women weren't allowed to serve on submarines. And that was just fine by the husbands.

But now the Silent Service is going coed, and inevitably there will be marriage-destroying affairs on submarines. Those who don't want to serve in Obama's submersible social laboratory can – and will – vote with their feet and leave the Navy. How many will leave the other forces if "Don't Ask, Don't Tell" is repealed?

Obama's push to repeal "Don't Ask, Don't Tell" got off to a running start when Adm. Mike Mullen, the chairman of the Joint Chiefs of Staff, told a Senate hearing that he

Why would anyone want to serve in an army whose leader believes it more important to be politically correct than to protect the lives of the soldiers?

was positive that the law should be repealed. He said, "No matter how I look at this issue, I cannot escape being troubled by the fact that we have in place a policy which forces young men and women to lie about who they are in order to defend their fellow citizens. For me personally, it comes down to integrity – theirs as individuals and ours as an institution."

Most of Obama's Pentagon seems as confused as Mullen about the difference between integrity and political correctness. But the push to repeal "Don't Ask, Don't Tell" hit a snag in the person of Marine Corps Commandant Gen. James Conway, who told the same committee that it would be a bad idea to repeal the law.

Conway retires in November 2010. Gates and Obama will be looking for another Marine, one who is more liberal and malleable, to take his place. It'll be pretty tough to find a Marine above the rank of lance corporal who's as malleable and liberal as Gates and Obama will want him to be.

Finally, pursuing Obama's agenda to cut the military budget, Gates is now saying that military pay and benefits will have to be frozen or cut.

At the end of 2009, about 19 percent of federal civilian employees were earning salaries of more than $100,000. And their job descriptions don't include having people shoot at them. An Army second lieutenant earns about $31,000 a year. An E-5 sergeant earns $28,000. Whose pay needs to be frozen or cut? Why not just fire 20 percent of all federal civilian workers?

Repealing "Don't Ask, Don't Tell," allowing women to serve on submarines, and attacking the pay and benefits our troops receive are the actions of an administration that wants to reduce our military capability, not enhance it.

Conclusion

We are a nation at war, governed by a man who evidently believes that the world would be a more peaceful place if the United States were unable and unwilling to affect the tide of events. He and his defense secretary are working diligently to ensure that this belief becomes reality.

They suffer from what Winston Churchill called the "unwisdom" that affected Europe and the United States between World Wars I and II. He wrote, in the first volume of *The Second World War*:

> *It is difficult to find a parallel to the unwisdom of the British and weakness of the French Governments . . . in this disastrous period. Nor can the United States escape the censure of history. Absorbed in their own affairs and all the abounding interests, activities and accidents of a free*

community, they simply gaped at the vast changes which were taking place in Europe, and imagined they were no concern of theirs.

Now we have precisely the kind of government he chastised, consumed by its domestic spending spree and hyperkinetic growth of government. President Obama and his cabinet – especially Defense Secretary Gates and Attorney General Holder – are willfully, even proudly, ignorant of the dangers we face.

Can we survive eight years of Barack Obama's unwisdom? Yes, and here's how.

First and foremost, we need to support our troops in every way possible, starting with pay raises – not cuts – across the board. To pay for this, we can and should eliminate tens of thousands of civilian government jobs. Reverse the glandular growth of government that the Obama administration has forced upon us and impose an across-the-board budget cut of 20 percent on every federal agency. We could even cut 20 percent of the civilian employees in the Department of Defense without missing a beat.

Second, we need to cut back our national spending. Our economy is in a false recovery. Once the Bush tax cuts expire next year, we'll be back in a deeper, longer recession. Obama is willing to spend billions on any crazy idea as long as its only product is more red ink and bigger government. If Republicans regain control of either half of Congress, they have to stop the spending. No more bailouts of General Motors or Greece or whatever.

When we can, we need to elect a conservative Republican as president, not just another Republican establishmentarian who will follow in the footsteps of Bob Dole and John McCain. And he has to do two things. One, repeal every spending program enacted in the Obama years and enact the tax cuts that will kick-start our economy, commencing with a massive cut – 10 percent or more – to the capital gains tax. Two, restart the F-22 and DDG-1000 programs and begin long-range bomber and anti-satellite weapon programs, among others.

There is, among America's engineering

and science community, another generation of technology jumpers like the late Ben Rich. Fund them, let them create jobs, and get out of their way. Our economy will rebuild itself before our eyes, and our nation – and the free world – will be safer for it.

First American edition published in 2010 by Encounter Books,
an activity of Encounter for Culture and Education, Inc.,
a nonprofit, tax exempt corporation.
Encounter Books website address: www.encounterbooks.com

Manufactured in the United States and printed on
acid-free paper. The paper used in this publication meets
the minimum requirements of ANSI/NISO Z39.48–1992
(R 1997) (*Permanence of Paper*).

FIRST AMERICAN EDITION

LIBRARY OF CONGRESS CATALOGING-IN-PUBLICATION DATA

Babbin, Jed L.
How Obama is transforming America's military from superpower to
paper tiger / by Jed Babbin.
p.   cm. — (Encounter broadsides)
ISBN-13: 978-1-59403-514-2 (pbk. : alk. paper)
ISBN-10: 1-59403-514-8 (pbk. : alk. paper)
1. United States—Military policy—21st century. 2. Obama, Barack.
3. United States. Dept. of Defense—Appropriations and expenditures.
4. United States—Armed Forces—Appropriations and expenditures.
5. United States—Foreign relations—2009– 6. Sociology, Military—
United States. I. Title.
UA23.B13 2010
355'.033573—dc22
2010020747

10 9 8 7 6 5 4 3 2 1